Take a Sip, Take a Breath and Go....

A Companion Book for Exploring and Discovering
Your Own Journey Through Motherhood

Michaela S. Cox

ISBN: 978-1-67-521334-6

Download for Free
Words of Affirmation for Moms and Kids

Just to say thanks ever so very much for reading my book,
I would like to give you this free resource
for your journey ahead through motherhood

To Download Go To:

www.subscribepage.com/AJourneyThroughMotherhood

A Word of Dedication

I would like to dedicate this book to the following people:

To My Husband

I dedicate this book to my loving husband who always loved, encouraged and supported me in all that I did and do. He was by my side in all things and would always encourage me to follow my dreams. He was always rooting for me and cheering me on. I will always and forever love you my Love.

To my children

I dedicate this book to my precious babies they are my treasures. They are the very reasons why I am a mother and are my ticket to travel this journey of motherhood. If not for them I wouldn't be a mother, traveled this journey and had opportunity to experience, learn, grow and have this message to write and share.

To all mothers everywhere

I dedicate this book to all my fellow mamas and travelers through this journey we call motherhood. May we always continue on our journey learning, growing, taking our sips, breaths, and go forward doing our best for our babies and families.

Table of Contents

A Word from the Author

In 2010 after becoming a mommy for the first, I realized, learned and discovered numerous new things as a virginal new mom. During this time in my journey I lived in New Hampshire with my husband and we were 26 hours away from all our friends and family. Also, at this time I did't really have mommy girlfriends. Many times, I was just left with my own thought on my own journey as new mommy. These learned lessons, observations, reflections, discoveries and experiences I was having prompted me to start to write Take a Sip, Take a Breath and Go…. A Journey Through Motherhood. In that book I simply just presented my feelings, thoughts, experiences, and observations that I had and have gone through since becoming a new mama. I was mostly virginal as a mama, and starting my learning and growing in my journey through my motherhood. I wish only to share my thoughts, feelings, and observations that I have gained and come to as I have traveled and keep moving forward as a mommy. I don't have all the answers, and I'm not perfect. Far from it. I wish only for my mommy food for thought to be shared and hopefully to help my fellow travelers along their journey as mamas. There is something to be said for not traveling alone, and knowing that others are going through it and doing the same. I think what brought me most to this place as an author and a mama is that the hardest thing was for me as a new mama was being so far from all my friends and not having anyone to talk to and share in my journey. I wish to share mine with other fellow mamas. I strive only to give my fellow travelers a place and space of freedom to explore as they continue on their journey as mamas. As fellow mamas traveling through this journey of motherhood, let's together learn to take our sips, our breaths, and go forward growing and journeying together through this thing we call motherhood journey of a lifetime. This book is a campaign to Take a Sip, Take a Breath and Go.... A Journey Through Motherhood. As I have traveled my own journey through motherhood for the last nine years I have had many questions, learned lessons and experiences. Each of these have taught me much and helped me grow much as a mommy. I have discovered much along the way. I hope and know that I will continue to do so as I keep traveling this journey that we call motherhood. As I have discovered much I want each you to have the same opportunity to make your own discoveries as you each travel on your own journey through motherhood. So consider these questions as much food for your thought as you continue to travel through your motherhood. May you keep taking your sips, breaths and go forward in your journey. Happy traveling.

How to Use This Book

In this book you will see that it is broken down into 37 discoveries (chapters) Each discover has a handful of questions for your consideration. There is space for you to have the freedom to explore, reflect and discover your own journey as a mommy. Use this space to have the freedom to express your own thoughts, reflections and observations of your own journey as a mom. Reflect on what your journey has been like and what it for you to be a mom and traveling this journey. Give yourself the freedom to take time to take your sips, take your breaths to sit and relax and as you reflect about your own motherhood journey. What have you learned and discovered. How have you changed or transformed. What have you observed and experienced. How have you grown in your motherhood. What does your motherhood mean to you. Feel free to learn from your journey, give yourself the grace you deserves when in the mommy valley moments and celebrate your mommy mountaintop moment and victories. Give yourself the space, freedom and permission to do this so that you may continue traveling your journey as a mommy being, doing and giving your best self to your babies and family. Let's travel on my fellow mommies taking our sips and breathes.

Dirty Dishes prove I feed my family,
full trash cans prove I clean up after their mess,
messy floors prove that I let my children have fun,
piles of clean laundry prove I keep my family in clean
clothes
a wet bathroom proves that I bathe my children.
So next time you walk into my house and see a mess,
think twice before you judge.
—Anonymous

Motherhood is not a competition
to see who has the smartest kids,
the cleanest house,
the healthiest dinners,
or the nicest clothes
Motherhood is your journey with your children
—Dr.laura.com

Discoveries

My House of Cards in My Journey Through Motherhood

In your journey through motherhood consider much the house you wish to build for you, your babies and families. Just as our own houses are built with different material and components what are the materials and components you wish to use in building the your house in motherhood. What is the foundation you strive to be standing on and have your motherhood built on?

1.Is your house of cards of motherhood falling or standing tall, strong, and steady?

_____

_____

_____

_____

_____

_____

_____

_____

_____

_____

_____

_____

_____

_____

_____

_____

_____

2.If standing strong, what causes it to stand strong?

_____

_____

_____

_____

_____

_____

_____

_____

_____

_____

_____

_____

_____

_____

_____

_____

3.If falling, what causes it to be fragile?

_____

_____

_____

_____

_____

_____

_____

_____

_____

_____

_____

_____

_____

_____

_____

_____

_____

_____

4.What can you do in your journey to steady and give strength to your house of cards in motherhood?

_____

_____

_____

_____

_____

_____

_____

_____

_____

_____

_____

_____

_____

_____

_____

_____

_____

_____

5.What do you want your house of cards of motherhood to look like and be built upon?

_____

_____

_____

_____

_____

_____

_____

_____

_____

_____

_____

_____

_____

_____

_____

_____

Discovery 2
Take a Sip, Take a Breath, and Go....

Ponder and determine the value you find in taking time for yourself and for attending to your own needs of self care. Do you find those moments to slip away to give and do something for yourself worthwhile? Define in what way do you take your sips, and take your breaths? Imagine what it would be like for you, your babies and family if you didn't do this and then if you did take your sips and breaths.

1.In becoming a new mommy, what was the biggest change or difference for you?

_____

_____

_____

_____

_____

_____

_____

_____

_____

_____

_____

_____

_____

_____

_____

2.In your journey as a new mommy, what takes up the most of your time?

_____

_____

_____

_____

_____

_____

_____

_____

_____

_____

_____

_____

_____

_____

_____

_____

3.What is the hardest thing about becoming a new mommy?

_____

_____

_____

_____

_____

_____

_____

_____

_____

_____

_____

_____

_____

_____

_____

_____

4.What causes you to feel overwhelmed?

_____

_____

_____

_____

_____

_____

_____

_____

_____

_____

_____

_____

_____

_____

_____

_____

_____

5.For you as a new mommy, what would it mean to take a sip, take a breath, relax, and then go?

_____

_____

_____

_____

_____

_____

_____

_____

_____

_____

_____

_____

_____

_____

_____

_____

_____

_____

6.How can you carve out a few minutes (or more) to give yourself time for your sips and breaths to relax and go forward as the best mommy you can be?

_____

_____

_____

_____

_____

_____

_____

_____

_____

_____

_____

_____

_____

_____

_____

Discovery 3
I'm a Virgin, In Motherhood, That is

In becoming a new mom reflect on in what ways have you been a virgin in motherhood the most. What areas are or you feel that you are the most inexperienced in? In entering into motherhood what have been the areas in which you found to be new and uncharted waters in which you are traveling through?

1.In your virginity as a new mommy, what do you find to be the newest experience?

_____

_____

_____

_____

_____

_____

_____

_____

_____

_____

_____

_____

_____

_____

_____

_____

2.What is the biggest unknown in your new motherhood?

_____

_____

_____

_____

_____

_____

_____

_____

_____

_____

_____

_____

_____

_____

_____

_____

3.How can you go forward to swim in these new uncharted
waters of motherhood?

_____

_____

_____

_____

_____

_____

_____

_____

_____

_____

_____

_____

_____

_____

_____

4.What can you do to grow into the ultimate experienced mommy?

_____

_____

_____

_____

_____

_____

_____

_____

_____

_____

_____

_____

_____

_____

_____

_____

Discovery 4

Motherhood: Does It Come With an Instruction Manual and Where Is Mine?

In your journey so far as a new mommy think on what do you wish you had a road map for with the directions or instructions for following as you travel this new journey. What area would you find it most helpful to haven instructions for? Do you feel or think it would have be better to have a ready made and given manual with our journey mapped out step by step as mommies?

1.How do you, as a mommy, find your way through motherhood without an instruction manual?

_____

_____

_____

_____

_____

_____

_____

_____

_____

_____

_____

_____

_____

_____

_____

_____

2.Where are you to find your instructions as to how to be a mommy?

_____

_____

_____

_____

_____

_____

_____

_____

_____

_____

_____

_____

_____

_____

_____

3.What instructions do you write for yourself, your child, and your family?

_____

_____

_____

_____

_____

_____

_____

_____

_____

_____

_____

_____

_____

_____

_____

_____

By Right of Birth, I Enter into Motherhood

Consider the path in which you enter into motherhood. How do you feel about your own method or path into motherhood? Do you think different paths into motherhood make you or any of our fellow travelers less of a mommy compared to other mamas? What gives us our ticket of entrance into motherhood.

1.What was the path that you traveled to start your journey through motherhood?

_____

_____

_____

_____

_____

_____

_____

_____

_____

_____

_____

_____

_____

_____

_____

_____

_____

2.What do you define as giving birth?

_____

_____

_____

_____

_____

_____

_____

_____

_____

_____

_____

_____

_____

_____

_____

_____

_____

_____

3.What do you define as the path that a woman takes to enter into motherhood?

_____

_____

_____

_____

_____

_____

_____

_____

_____

_____

_____

_____

_____

_____

_____

_____

_____

4. Does your path you traveled to enter into motherhood make any less of a mother than another who traveled a different path to motherhood?

_____

_____

_____

_____

_____

_____

_____

_____

_____

_____

_____

_____

_____

_____

_____

_____

_____

5.What Defines motherhood and what it is to be mother?

_____

_____

_____

_____

_____

_____

_____

_____

_____

_____

_____

_____

_____

_____

_____

_____

_____

6.Do the different paths taken to enter into motherhood change the journey of motherhood for each us as individual travelers of motherhood?

_____

_____

_____

_____

_____

_____

_____

_____

_____

_____

_____

_____

_____

_____

_____

_____

Discovery 6
The Breastfeeding Gestapo

This personal, imitate, and controversial topic of breasting feed/nursing seems to be fundamental to motherhood and our journey as mamas. Consider the importance of this topic for your own journey. Think on what you know is best for you and your baby. Know that whatever you chose that you are doing what is best and right for you and your baby. Know whatever you choose it's your journey and yours alone as you travel through motherhood.

1. In choosing what to do, consider what you think you want as the mommy of your baby.

_____

_____

_____

_____

_____

_____

_____

_____

_____

_____

_____

_____

_____

_____

_____

_____

_____

2. In making a decision, think about what methods of feeding makes you comfortable.

_____

_____

_____

_____

_____

_____

_____

_____

_____

_____

_____

_____

_____

_____

_____

_____

_____

3.In choosing, think about what is best for you, your child, and your family.

_____

_____

_____

_____

_____

_____

_____

_____

_____

_____

_____

_____

_____

_____

_____

_____

4.In your decision-making process, consider that you are ultimately the most experienced in matters regarding your child and family.

_____

_____

_____

_____

_____

_____

_____

_____

_____

_____

_____

_____

_____

_____

_____

_____

Nipples–Mine or the Nipple of a Bottle

Reflect on is this a complex or simple issue of you in your journey. Consider your countless choices. It's amazing just how many choices we are faced with as moms. Consider your own choices. Be confident in what you choose. Trust your voice and know you are doing what is best for you and your baby.

1.In regard to how you choose to feed your baby, what makes the most sense and works the best for you, your baby, and your family?

_____

_____

_____

_____

_____

_____

_____

_____

_____

_____

_____

_____

_____

_____

_____

_____

_____

_____

2.In making these constant choices, choose that which doesn't consume you as the mommy.

_____

_____

_____

_____

_____

_____

_____

_____

_____

_____

_____

_____

_____

_____

_____

_____

_____

3.In considering your choices, what do you, as the ultimate expert, consider the best choice for you, your baby, and family?

_____

_____

_____

_____

_____

_____

_____

_____

_____

_____

_____

_____

_____

_____

_____

_____

_____

_____

Moving On Up In the World of the Girlfriends

On your journey as a mom think on all the changes you have gone through as a woman during pregnancy. Contemplate all the different changes you have encountered since becoming a mommy. In what ways have you changed the most. What changes have you find to be the most challenging? These change you have experienced has it been for the worse or for the better? How have these changes shaped you as a woman and a new mom?

1.What were the biggest or most significant changes you went through as a new mommy?

_____

_____

_____

_____

_____

_____

_____

_____

_____

_____

_____

_____

_____

_____

_____

2.In what ways did your life change the most as a new mommy?

_____

_____

_____

_____

_____

_____

_____

_____

_____

_____

_____

_____

_____

_____

_____

_____

_____

3.How did you adjust to all these changes?

_____

_____

_____

_____

_____

_____

_____

_____

_____

_____

_____

_____

_____

_____

_____

_____

4.What ways can you find or use to bounce back from this complete transformation and get back to you again in all senses?

_____

_____

_____

_____

_____

_____

_____

_____

_____

_____

_____

_____

_____

_____

_____

_____

_____

To Feed or to Pee

In your journey of motherhood how has it forced you to consider your choices and how you make choices since entering motherhood? Ponder how and what you prioritize now. Have you had different priorities since entering into motherhood. How do you make the choice in what to prioritize now as a mom? What is your top or number one priorities now since entering motherhood?

1.As a new mommy, how do you decide what needs to be addressed and attended to?

_____

_____

_____

_____

_____

_____

_____

_____

_____

_____

_____

_____

_____

_____

_____

2.What or whose needs do you make a priority?

_____

_____

_____

_____

_____

_____

_____

_____

_____

_____

_____

_____

_____

_____

_____

_____

3.In deciding this, how do you balance the all the new needs of motherhood?

_____

_____

_____

_____

_____

_____

_____

_____

_____

_____

_____

_____

_____

_____

_____

_____

_____

Discovery 10
My Never-Ending Rollercoaster Ride of Hormones

Since entering into the journey of motherhood consider what has your ride been like in motherhood. What has made it a crazy ride or a smooth ride? Has your own ride been more like a rollercoaster ride? How do you find the balance as a new mommy on this new ride of motherhood?

1.What was the most significant change for you as a new mommy?

_____

_____

_____

_____

_____

_____

_____

_____

_____

_____

_____

_____

_____

_____

_____

2.How does you survive the ups and downs of this rollercoaster ride?

_____

_____

_____

_____

_____

_____

_____

_____

_____

_____

_____

_____

_____

_____

_____

_____

3.How do you get yourself off this ride and back to normal?

_____

_____

_____

_____

_____

_____

_____

_____

_____

_____

_____

_____

_____

_____

_____

_____

4.How can you find your center and balance again as a new mommy?

_____

_____

_____

_____

_____

_____

_____

_____

_____

_____

_____

_____

_____

_____

_____

_____

Minute to Minute In the Life of My Day As a Mommy

Time is always of the essence even more so in motherhood. How did you use your time before becoming a mommy? Consider how you use your time now as a mom since entering into motherhood compare to before. What do you find that takes up your time? How do you use your time now? How have you adjusted what you spend your time on as you travel as a mommy?

1.As a mommy, how do you spend your time?

_____

_____

_____

_____

_____

_____

_____

_____

_____

_____

_____

_____

_____

_____

_____

_____

_____

2.What is a priority for you in the use of your time?

_____

_____

_____

_____

_____

_____

_____

_____

_____

_____

_____

_____

_____

_____

_____

_____

_____

3.How do you mange or juggle the new demands on your time as a new mommy?

_____

_____

_____

_____

_____

_____

_____

_____

_____

_____

_____

_____

_____

_____

_____

4.What tools do you use to manage and juggle the demands on your time?

_____

_____

_____

_____

_____

_____

_____

_____

_____

_____

_____

_____

_____

_____

_____

_____

Discovery 12
In Just a Minute, My Precious, Sweet Baby Girl

In motherhood consider much how you spend your days. What take up your time? How do you spend the minutes and hours of you days? Do you think what you spend your time on as a mommy is waste of your time? Do you feel that what you spend your time on as a mama is worthy of your time? Do your children and families think that your time spent is a worth or wasteful of usage of your valuable time as a mama?

1.What do you choose to spend your time on?

_____

_____

_____

_____

_____

_____

_____

_____

_____

_____

_____

_____

_____

_____

_____

2.Do you consider it a worthy or wasteful use of your time?

_____

_____

_____

_____

_____

_____

_____

_____

_____

_____

_____

_____

_____

_____

_____

_____

_____

3.Would your child/children consider it a worthy or wasteful use of your time?

_____

_____

_____

_____

_____

_____

_____

_____

_____

_____

_____

_____

_____

_____

_____

_____

4.How do you want to use and spend your seconds, minutes, hours, and days of your motherhood?

_____

_____

_____

_____

_____

_____

_____

_____

_____

_____

_____

_____

_____

_____

_____

_____

Sleep, Snacks, Sips, Soaks, and Sex:
Catch While You Can

In motherhood is seems like the days are long and years are short. It seems as some days goes slower than a snail's pace and other faster than a road runner. Do you as a mom take your sips and breaths? Do you as a mama make sure you get your soaks, snacks and beauty sleep? How do you fine the time do to the things for yourself? in what ways to you make sure you get to catch moments to do these things and take the much needed moments for yourself?

1.As a mommy, in getting your sleep, snacks, sips, or soaks, which is most important?

_____

_____

_____

_____

_____

_____

_____

_____

_____

_____

_____

_____

_____

_____

_____

_____

2.As a mommy, should you have to choose between these things?

_____

_____

_____

_____

_____

_____

_____

_____

_____

_____

_____

_____

_____

_____

_____

_____

3. Why does getting these things as a mommy seem so elusive, a rare moment?

_____

_____

_____

_____

_____

_____

_____

_____

_____

_____

_____

_____

_____

_____

_____

_____

4.How will you find the moment to take your sips, snacks, sleeps, and soaks?

_____

_____

_____

_____

_____

_____

_____

_____

_____

_____

_____

_____

_____

_____

_____

_____

My Me O'clock Time

In motherhood when checking off your to do list consider what takes up the minutes and hours of your day as mom? How do you spend your O'clocks? Are there any Clocks for you? How do you carve some minutes to give you your Me O'clock time? How do you spend your Me O'clocks in your days as a mommy?

1.What does Me O'clock mean to you as a mommy?

_____

_____

_____

_____

_____

_____

_____

_____

_____

_____

_____

_____

_____

_____

_____

2.What would you do with your "me" time?

_____

_____

_____

_____

_____

_____

_____

_____

_____

_____

_____

_____

_____

_____

_____

_____

3.How would you often would you like to have Me O'clock?

_____

_____

_____

_____

_____

_____

_____

_____

_____

_____

_____

_____

_____

_____

_____

_____

4.What can you do to ensure you get and take your Me O'clock
moments?

_____

_____

_____

_____

_____

_____

_____

_____

_____

_____

_____

_____

_____

_____

_____

_____

Murphy's Laws of Motherhood

In life there seems to be examples of Murphy's Law that occur in our lives on a daily basis. In days in the life of being a mom and with our babies this seems to be even more common. Whether instances of Murphy laws is a source frustration or interesting, humorous incidents in motherhood consider how much this plays a role in your daily life in motherhood. Consider if more on the frustrating side what might be helpful in lessening the pressure or load of the effect of the Murphy law of motherhood

1.What are the Murphy's Laws of your Motherhood?

_____

_____

_____

_____

_____

_____

_____

_____

_____

_____

_____

_____

_____

_____

_____

_____

_____

2.What is the cause of the epidemic of the Murphy's Laws in your motherhood?

_____

_____

_____

_____

_____

_____

_____

_____

_____

_____

_____

_____

_____

_____

_____

3.What remedies would you use to vaccinate against the Murphy's Laws of your motherhood?

_____

_____

_____

_____

_____

_____

_____

_____

_____

_____

_____

_____

_____

_____

_____

_____

The Small and Simple Saving Graces of My Motherhood

Its interesting that culturally its said not to sweat the small stuff which very much may be true. it's often times the small things that can make all the difference in the world. In motherhood the case is no different. Consider what small things have been your saving graces in you days a mom? Consider how you can find saving graces? How do these small and simple things provide you your saving grace in your motherhood?

1.When in a day in the life of a mommy do you need some saving graces?

_____

_____

_____

_____

_____

_____

_____

_____

_____

_____

_____

_____

_____

_____

_____

_____

2.What is the reason for the need for your daily saving grace?

_____

_____

_____

_____

_____

_____

_____

_____

_____

_____

_____

_____

_____

_____

_____

_____

_____

3.What would be your saving grace?

_____

_____

_____

_____

_____

_____

_____

_____

_____

_____

_____

_____

_____

_____

_____

_____

4.How can you find or obtain the much-needed daily saving grace as a mommy?

_____

_____

_____

_____

_____

_____

_____

_____

_____

_____

_____

_____

_____

_____

_____

I Have My Moments, Don't We All?

Life is made up of multiple, diverse, elective various types of moments. Some moments are good, some are bad and many in between. Equally motherhood is made up the same divers range of moments. Also we as women and mommies we experience and our journeys are made up by the same range of moments. Consider what types of moments do you have more of. Consider what moments do you get to have in your motherhood and after becoming a mommy.

1.When do you have your own mommy moments?

_____

_____

_____

_____

_____

_____

_____

_____

_____

_____

_____

_____

_____

_____

_____

_____

2.Is your mommy moment in the mommy valley, and what caused it?

_____

_____

_____

_____

_____

_____

_____

_____

_____

_____

_____

_____

_____

_____

_____

_____

3.Is your mommy moment on the mommy mountaintop, and what caused it?

_____

_____

_____

_____

_____

_____

_____

_____

_____

_____

_____

_____

_____

_____

_____

4.How do you achieve more of your mommy mountaintop moments and have less of you mommy valley moments?

_____

_____

_____

_____

_____

_____

_____

_____

_____

_____

_____

_____

_____

_____

_____

_____

_____

Mother and Child—Learning and Growing Hand in Hand

In life we learn much from the all the things we experience. Our experiences teach us much and help us to grow as we travel along our journey. I have not known any other experience that does this more than motherhood. It's unclear as to who learns or teaches more us or our children. Consider what you have learned since starting your journey as a mother. Consider what you have and want to teach your children and what they are learning.

1.What does walking hand in hand with your baby/babies mean to you as a mommy?

_____

_____

_____

_____

_____

_____

_____

_____

_____

_____

_____

_____

_____

_____

_____

_____

2.What do you want to teach, exemplify, and instill in your baby/babies?

_____

_____

_____

_____

_____

_____

_____

_____

_____

_____

_____

_____

_____

_____

_____

_____

3.What has your baby/babies taught you as you walk hand in hand along this journey?

_____

_____

_____

_____

_____

_____

_____

_____

_____

_____

_____

_____

_____

_____

_____

_____

4.How will the manner in which you walk hand in hand with your baby/babies impact or influence your continued journey together?

_____

_____

_____

_____

_____

_____

_____

_____

_____

_____

_____

_____

_____

_____

_____

First, Foremost, and Forever, I am Mama

Motherhood everything changes. Motherhood changes us as women. We learn just exactly, how extensively, expansively, and all encompassing motherhood changes us. Motherhood also has a way of affecting what becomes priority. Motherhood has a way to altering what we see is important in life.

Motherhood influences how we see ourselves as women and as mamas. Consider how you have changed. Consider how you see yourself after becoming a mother. Consider what you value and define as priority in your motherhood.

1.In becoming a mommy, how have you and your life changed?

_____

_____

_____

_____

_____

_____

_____

_____

_____

_____

_____

_____

_____

_____

_____

_____

2.How do you see yourself now after becoming a mommy?

_____

_____

_____

_____

_____

_____

_____

_____

_____

_____

_____

_____

_____

_____

_____

_____

_____

3.What does being first, foremost, and forever Mama mean to you as a new mommy?

_____

_____

_____

_____

_____

_____

_____

_____

_____

_____

_____

_____

_____

_____

_____

_____

_____

4.What do you do to ensure that you are first, foremost, and forever Mama?

_____

_____

_____

_____

_____

_____

_____

_____

_____

_____

_____

_____

_____

_____

_____

_____

My Manners in Motherhood Matter

We are all taught to mind your manners. We learned that manners matter. In becoming mothers ourselves we continue to teach and instill these valuable lessons in our babies. If manners matter in life and we want our babies to learn this then how much more should we remember our manners matter in our motherhood. Consider how you want to demonstrate and mind your manners in your motherhood. Consider what manners in your motherhood matter.

1.Do your manners as a mommy matter?

_____

_____

_____

_____

_____

_____

_____

_____

_____

_____

_____

_____

_____

_____

_____

_____

_____

_____

2.What manners matter the most to you as a mommy?

_____

_____

_____

_____

_____

_____

_____

_____

_____

_____

_____

_____

_____

_____

_____

_____

3.Which manners do you wish to teach, exemplify, and instill in your baby/babies?

_____

_____

_____

_____

_____

_____

_____

_____

_____

_____

_____

_____

_____

_____

_____

_____

_____

_____

4.How will you make manners matter in motherhood for you and your baby/babies?

_____

_____

_____

_____

_____

_____

_____

_____

_____

_____

_____

_____

_____

_____

_____

Making Lemonade Out of the Lemons in My Motherhood

In life one of the sweetest things is and nothing can be as good as a cold glass of lemonade. Lemonade is made with sugar and lemons. Often times what life hands us isn't so sweet. Many times what motherhood gives us is not sweet lemonade but lemons. In these times we have a choice in life to deal and sit with the lemons handed to us or a choice to make something sweet out of those lemons and turn them into lemonade. When life and motherhood gives us lemons consider what you as a mother want to do with your motherhood lemons. Consider what you wish your babies to learn about the lemons of life and how to deal with the lemons they are handled.

1.What lemons do you have or have you been given in your journey as a mommy?

_____

_____

_____

_____

_____

_____

_____

_____

_____

_____

_____

_____

_____

_____

_____

_____

2.What do you choose to do with your lemons as a mommy?

_____

_____

_____

_____

_____

_____

_____

_____

_____

_____

_____

_____

_____

_____

_____

_____

_____

3.How do you make lemonade out of the lemons of your motherhood?

_____

_____

_____

_____

_____

_____

_____

_____

_____

_____

_____

_____

_____

_____

_____

4.How do you enjoy glass or pitcher of lemonade in your journey as a mommy?

_____

_____

_____

_____

_____

_____

_____

_____

_____

_____

_____

_____

_____

_____

_____

The Punishing Abuses and the Awarding Privileges of Motherhood

In motherhood we can experience a diverse myriad of things. We can also have a variety of different moments with our babies. Some moments can feel like we are getting abused and other feel like we are getting the greatest award that feel as if we are getting a most high privilege. What feels as if it is a punishing abuse to you in your motherhood? What gives a moment of great awarding privilege as a momma?

1.In your own journey as a mommy, what are some of the punishing abuses?

_____

_____

_____

_____

_____

_____

_____

_____

_____

_____

_____

_____

_____

_____

_____

_____

2.In your own journey as a mommy, what are some of the awarding privileges?

_____

_____

_____

_____

_____

_____

_____

_____

_____

_____

_____

_____

_____

_____

_____

_____

3.How do you find your own awarding privileges as a mommy?

_____

_____

_____

_____

_____

_____

_____

_____

_____

_____

_____

_____

_____

_____

_____

_____

_____

_____

4.How do you use the punishing abuses and the awarding privileges in your journey through motherhood?

_____

_____

_____

_____

_____

_____

_____

_____

_____

_____

_____

_____

_____

_____

_____

_____

Affirming Moments of Achievements and Awards in Motherhood

In motherhood we can equally have moments that are very affirming. These moments can feel as we are achieving much in our journey as mommies. It can be a mountain top mommy moment. For you as a mommy what gives your mommy mountain top moment of achievement is it through watching your babies have milestone or a goal accomplished. Is it something you feel you have conquered as a mom or that you feel you have made great strides in becoming less virginal and more your own mommy expert.

1.As a mommy, what do you define as an affirming moment?

_____

_____

_____

_____

_____

_____

_____

_____

_____

_____

_____

_____

_____

_____

_____

_____

2.As a mommy, what do you see as an achievement in your motherhood?

_____

_____

_____

_____

_____

_____

_____

_____

_____

_____

_____

_____

_____

_____

_____

_____

_____

3.How can you, in your motherhood, achieve more moments of success and affirmation?

_____

_____

_____

_____

_____

_____

_____

_____

_____

_____

_____

_____

_____

_____

_____

_____

WOW! Am I Mommy or an Acrobat Now?

Acrobats can do amazing and incredible things, acts and tricks. Motherhood often times can feel as if we are acrobats walking a tight rope, doing insane juggling acts, pulling off all sorts of crazy stunts and balancing acts in our days of our lives as mommies. What do you juggle in your day as a mommy What tricks or stunts do you have to perform. Consider what helps you keep your balance as a mommy. What medal would you be awarded for your juggling act? What do you define as achieving your mommy medal?

1.As a mommy, what has been thrown into your mix that you have to juggle?

_____

_____

_____

_____

_____

_____

_____

_____

_____

_____

_____

_____

_____

_____

_____

2.How do you define your juggling abilities as a mommy?

_____

_____

_____

_____

_____

_____

_____

_____

_____

_____

_____

_____

_____

_____

_____

_____

3.How do you find the balance in your juggling act of motherhood?

_____

_____

_____

_____

_____

_____

_____

_____

_____

_____

_____

_____

_____

_____

_____

Discovery 25
The Experts Say....

In our culture we are surrounded and engulfed by information and experts. This is even more the case in our journeys as mommies. In your mommy journey what areas do you seek expert advice? What experts to you look too? Do you feel bombarded with the voices of the experts? Consider this do you think of yourself as your own expert? Do you feel confident in your own voice of expertise to guide your own journey through motherhood as the mommy to your babies?

1.How do you see yourself as a mommy: virgin or expert?

_____

_____

_____

_____

_____

_____

_____

_____

_____

_____

_____

_____

_____

_____

_____

_____

2.When becoming a new mommy, what were you most virginal in?

_____

_____

_____

_____

_____

_____

_____

_____

_____

_____

_____

_____

_____

_____

_____

3.As a mommy, what are you the most expert in?

_____

_____

_____

_____

_____

_____

_____

_____

_____

_____

_____

_____

_____

_____

_____

_____

4.How have you, in your journey as a mommy, become the expert in your child/children and family?

_____

_____

_____

_____

_____

_____

_____

_____

_____

_____

_____

_____

_____

_____

_____

Discovery 26
No More Commentary
From the Peanut Galleries

In the beginning of one's journey into motherhood there seems to be an endless sea of a chorus of voices giving advice or commentary whether requested or not. The chorus can be a very opinionated and noisy chorus. This chorus can either be out of tune with us as mommies or cause us to feel out tune with our own voice and journey. Do you feel as if you be drowned by the chorus of commentary? Consider this how do you find, hear and follow your own true voice of guidance for you, your motherhood and your babies? Remember each of us are on our journey that we have to follow and find our own way in our motherhood for ourselves and our babies.

1.As a mommy, do you feel lost or overwhelmed by the constant sea of commentary?

_____

_____

_____

_____

_____

_____

_____

_____

_____

_____

_____

_____

_____

_____

_____

_____

2.How can you, as a mommy, find your own voice amidst all the chatter of commentary?

_____

_____

_____

_____

_____

_____

_____

_____

_____

_____

_____

_____

_____

_____

_____

_____

3.How will you silence the chatter and commentary to find, learn, and trust your own expert voice for you, your babies, and family?

_____

_____

_____

_____

_____

_____

_____

_____

_____

_____

_____

_____

_____

_____

_____

_____

Discovery 27
Judge Not Lest You Be Judged
As a Mother

There are some well know cultural expressions that reference how we should or not respond to the actions or lives of the people around us. You have heard it said those in glasses houses shouldn't throw stones. Also it has been stated that judge not lest you be judged. The journey of motherhood is the greatest journey of a lifetime and yet its also the hardest, most demanding and most challenging journey. Consider this who is the mom to your child? You and you alone are who and what is best and right for you and your babies.

Give yourself as a mommy much grace and permission to travel your own journey learning, discovering and growing in your motherhood

1.As a mommy, in what ways do you feel judged?

_____

_____

_____

_____

_____

_____

_____

_____

_____

_____

_____

_____

_____

_____

_____

_____

2.For what do you feel you are being judged?

_____

_____

_____

_____

_____

_____

_____

_____

_____

_____

_____

_____

_____

_____

_____

_____

_____

3.How do you see yourself in your own glass of motherhood?

_____

_____

_____

_____

_____

_____

_____

_____

_____

_____

_____

_____

_____

_____

_____

_____

_____

_____

4.How will you give yourself the space and freedom to learn, discover, explore, and go forward in your journey as a mommy, free from the voices of judgment?

_____

_____

_____

_____

_____

_____

_____

_____

_____

_____

_____

_____

_____

_____

_____

The Golden Ruler of My Motherhood

In our culture we are always measuring any and everything that can possibly be measured. There are different things to be measured and there are different ways to do so. Rules are a great meter for measuring. We are also always seeing how we measure up. In motherhood what do you define as your rules for measuring up? What do you compare your self too? Consider this what should be and how you define and measure yourself and your motherhood?

1.As a mommy, what do you define as your golden rules?

_____

_____

_____

_____

_____

_____

_____

_____

_____

_____

_____

_____

_____

_____

_____

_____

2.What will be the golden ruler of your motherhood?

_____

_____

_____

_____

_____

_____

_____

_____

_____

_____

_____

_____

_____

_____

_____

_____

_____

3.How do you chose to be measured as a mommy?

_____

_____

_____

_____

_____

_____

_____

_____

_____

_____

_____

_____

_____

_____

_____

_____

I Am Now and Forever Mama

Some things and journeys in life change us forever. These journeys forever change and there is no going back to what was before. Once entering your motherhood how did you change? Consider how do you identify yourself after motherhood? Consider what defines you now since becoming a mommy?

1.After becoming a mommy, in what moments did you know you were now and forever mama?

_____

_____

_____

_____

_____

_____

_____

_____

_____

_____

_____

_____

_____

_____

_____

2.As you continue as a mommy, what moments do you look forward to the most?

_____

_____

_____

_____

_____

_____

_____

_____

_____

_____

_____

_____

_____

_____

_____

_____

_____

3.How will you always remember and hang on to those "I am now and forever Mama" moments?

_____

_____

_____

_____

_____

_____

_____

_____

_____

_____

_____

_____

_____

_____

_____

Discovery 30
My Motherhood Matters

In life many things matter and what matters often is determined and defined by what we value and make a priority. We all define these things differently. Consider after becoming a mom what has become important? In your motherhood what do you define as mattering most? Consider this does your motherhood matter?

1.Does your motherhood matter?

_____

_____

_____

_____

_____

_____

_____

_____

_____

_____

_____

_____

_____

_____

_____

_____

_____

2.In journeying through motherhood, what matters the most?

_____

_____

_____

_____

_____

_____

_____

_____

_____

_____

_____

_____

_____

_____

_____

_____

3.What do you define as mattering in your motherhood?

_____

_____

_____

_____

_____

_____

_____

_____

_____

_____

_____

_____

_____

_____

_____

_____

_____

Savoring the Seasons and Sands of Time In My Motherhood

In life there are many different season some that are sour and other seasons that are so sweet we savor them. Consider what seasons as a mommy have been sour. What have been the sweetest seasons of your journey as a new mommy? What seasons of your motherhood you have and you will savored forever as you continue to travel your own journey as a mommy?

1.What seasons have you experienced as a mommy on your own journey?

_____

_____

_____

_____

_____

_____

_____

_____

_____

_____

_____

_____

_____

_____

_____

2.What have you done with the sands of time in the various seasons of your journey?

_____

_____

_____

_____

_____

_____

_____

_____

_____

_____

_____

_____

_____

_____

_____

3.As a mommy, have you counted the days or made your days as a mommy count?

_____

_____

_____

_____

_____

_____

_____

_____

_____

_____

_____

_____

_____

_____

_____

_____

Discovery 32
Memorable Moments of My Motherhood

Life is made up of memorable moments. Our journey is made by moments that we will remember always. We have a lifetime of moments that we want to cherish and tuck away in the scrapbook of our hearts that we take with us always as we travel our life's journey. Consider what are the moments in your motherhood that are memorable and that you will take with you, cherish always and are the treasures that you will keep in the scrapbook of your heart and to take with you all along your journey as a mommy to your babies.

1.As a mommy, what do you defines as a memorable moment?

_____

_____

_____

_____

_____

_____

_____

_____

_____

_____

_____

_____

_____

_____

_____

2.Which moments of your motherhood are the most memorable for you?

_____

_____

_____

_____

_____

_____

_____

_____

_____

_____

_____

_____

_____

_____

_____

_____

_____

3.Which memorable moments of your motherhood will you always treasure, tuck away and use to fill your mommy scrapbook and heart for a lifetime?

_____

_____

_____

_____

_____

_____

_____

_____

_____

_____

_____

_____

_____

_____

_____

_____

My Plate Full of Spaghetti as a Mommy

A plate full of delicious pasta can be quite messy. Even messier can be trying to eat that huge loaded mound of crazy spaghetti. In motherhood we have so much that goes on. How much fuller our mommy plates? Consider how much and how full your mommy plate is filled with noddles. What noddles make up the mommy spaghetti that you have on you plate? Consider how do you mange, process and digest the spaghetti of your motherhood?

1.How messy is the plate of spaghetti of your motherhood?

_____

_____

_____

_____

_____

_____

_____

_____

_____

_____

_____

_____

_____

_____

_____

_____

2.What causes your plate of spaghetti to get entangled?

_____

_____

_____

_____

_____

_____

_____

_____

_____

_____

_____

_____

_____

_____

_____

_____

_____

3.What tools or ways do you use to solve the tangled mess of your plate of spaghetti of motherhood?

_____

_____

_____

_____

_____

_____

_____

_____

_____

_____

_____

_____

_____

_____

_____

_____

4.How can you, going forward in your journey as a mommy, prevent future entanglements of the spaghetti of your motherhood?

_____

_____

_____

_____

_____

_____

_____

_____

_____

_____

_____

_____

_____

_____

_____

_____

_____

My Evolutionary Journey as a Mommy

The idea of evolving is about change. Life is a stream of constant change and evolving. Motherhood is one of the biggest if not the biggest change one can go through in one's life. Consider how have you evolved since becoming a mommy. How much have you evolved in your own journey as a mother?

1.In journeying as a mommy, do you see yourself as virgin or an expert?

_____

_____

_____

_____

_____

_____

_____

_____

_____

_____

_____

_____

_____

_____

_____

_____

2.Through your journey as a mommy, how have you seen yourself evolve?

_____

_____

_____

_____

_____

_____

_____

_____

_____

_____

_____

_____

_____

_____

_____

3.What have been the steps of evolving as a mommy?

_____

_____

_____

_____

_____

_____

_____

_____

_____

_____

_____

_____

_____

_____

_____

4.What will help you to continue to evolve as you journey through your motherhood?

_____

_____

_____

_____

_____

_____

_____

_____

_____

_____

_____

_____

_____

_____

_____

_____

My Rainbow of True Colors as a Mommy

Rainbows are one of the most beautiful and brilliant aspects of nature. They represent the brilliant colors in the world. We all have beauty in us that represents our true colors. No matter how hard and deeply buried our truly brilliantly beautiful rainbow we have to find, believe and let our true colors shine. What does your true colors say about you? What are your true colors in your motherhood? Consider what colors you want to shine before your babies.

1.What are your true colors as a mommy?

_____

_____

_____

_____

_____

_____

_____

_____

_____

_____

_____

_____

_____

_____

_____

_____

2.Do you show or let shine the brightness of your true colors in your rainbow?

_____

_____

_____

_____

_____

_____

_____

_____

_____

_____

_____

_____

_____

_____

_____

_____

_____

3.Do you show or let be known the darker colors in your rainbow?

_____

_____

_____

_____

_____

_____

_____

_____

_____

_____

_____

_____

_____

_____

_____

_____

4.How can you show and let shine for yourself, your baby/babies, and family the beautiful brilliance and brightness of the true colors of your rainbow?

_____

_____

_____

_____

_____

_____

_____

_____

_____

_____

_____

_____

_____

_____

_____

_____

_____

For Better or Worse, I am Mommy

In life there is and will be times of better and then times of worse. This is no less true or different in motherhood. Times in our journey as mommies can make us questions if being a mommy is for worse or better. What makes you feel it's for the worse? What makes you feel it's for the better? We do our best and we are the best for our babies.

1.Has your journey as a mommy been for the worse or the better?

_____

_____

_____

_____

_____

_____

_____

_____

_____

_____

_____

_____

_____

_____

_____

_____

_____

2.Do you feel as if you have made the best or worst choices?

_____

_____

_____

_____

_____

_____

_____

_____

_____

_____

_____

_____

_____

_____

_____

_____

_____

3.In the choices you make as a mommy, what are the right choices for you, your baby, and family?

_____

_____

_____

_____

_____

_____

_____

_____

_____

_____

_____

_____

_____

_____

_____

_____

4.In your journey, what have you discovered to know that no matter what comes, for worse or better, you are the best for you are the one and only that is first, foremost, and forever, Mama, and no one can do it like you do it for you are the mother of your baby?

_____

_____

_____

_____

_____

_____

_____

_____

_____

_____

_____

_____

_____

_____

The Lessons I Have Learned Journeying Through My Motherhood

Life is about discovering, knowledge and learning lessons. We strive to teach our babies and hope they learn the lessons we work to instill in them. Consider what lessons you have learned from the knowledge, discoveries you had in your journey in motherhood. Consider have you taught your babies more or have you learned more.

1.In your journey as a mommy, what lessons have you learned?

_____

_____

_____

_____

_____

_____

_____

_____

_____

_____

_____

_____

_____

_____

_____

2.In becoming a mommy, what has been the biggest or most influential lesson you have learned?

_____

_____

_____

_____

_____

_____

_____

_____

_____

_____

_____

_____

_____

_____

_____

_____

3.As a mommy, what lessons are most important that you want to exemplify, teach, and instill in your baby/babies?

_____

_____

_____

_____

_____

_____

_____

_____

_____

_____

_____

_____

_____

_____

_____

Appendices

- **Appendix A:** Parental Positives

- **Appendix B:** Ways to Take Our Sips, Breaths and Go....

- **Appendix C:** Resources for the Journey Ahead

Appendix A
Parental Positives

Purpose of Appendix A

Explore, Discovery, Learn and Journey through Your own Motherhood

The idea of my parental positives started in New Hampshire with my counselor that I was seeing at the time. I was in session having concerns and worries over how I was doing in my own journey as a mommy and I how I was feeling about how I was doing. So my therapist said when I was/have moments where I'm doubting myself, worried, concerned or feeling overwhelmed for me to think of some things I thought I did or do that we are good/green, right, positive and healthily things in my motherhood. I was told that anything could be put on the list it could be simple, small, big or complex and it didn't matter what it was as long as It was something I thought I was doing well or positive in my motherhood. So I made a list and this what I came up with at the time. In my moments of feeling stressed, worried, concerned and overwhelmed I would look at my list. My list would help me realized that yes I'm doing this right, I'm doing okay and I've got this. I challenge all my fellow travelers in motherhood to make your own list of parental positives. Make it your own and put whatever makes you feel or think that you are doing a good job, that is positive and healthy that you are doing in your motherhood for your babies. Let this list be what makes you feel as you got this and then continue going through your journey in motherhood.

The List of **My Parental Positives** for my own journey through Motherhood

1. I give my babies as many as possible kisses and hugs.

2. I snuggle and cuddle with my babies as much as possible.

3. I hold my babies as much as possible.

4. I affirm/complement/encourage my babies as much as possible.

5. I let my babies pick/make their own choices as much and when possible.

6. I give my babies chores they are expected to do daily and or weekly.

7. I give my babies weekly commission for their chores not an allowance and it's only given if chores are completed.

8. I make time for special time with each of my babies.

9. On weekends when home my babies get choice time for special time.

10. When possible and often as possible I do story time with my babies or family reading time together.

11. When possible and often as possible I do family movie/game night with my babies.

12. Weekly (to the best of my ability) I do family devotional together wth my babies.

13. My babies and I go to church together.

14. My babies and I say night time prayers and morning prayers before we start our days.

15. I talk with my babies about God and when they have questions I do my best to answer their questions.

16. In the summer I go swimming with my babies daily when weather permits.

17. My babies are provided with good and healthy food/drink choices.

18. Sweets, treats and desserts are limited expect for special occasions.

19. I have and enforce strict early bed times for my babies.

20. When my babies make bad choices I discuss and explain why that was a bad/red choice or ask them was that choice good/green or bad/red and why it was a bad or good choice.

21. When my babies make good/green choices I praise/applaud and encourage my babies making good choices

22. When my babies are in trouble I will say "that choice doesn't make mommy happy". I never ever equate their bad choices to my love or lack of love for them.

23. When my babies are in trouble I always follow up with My love will never ever change and will always and forever love you no matter what.

24. TV and screen time I focus on quality and making good strict choices of the selection of what is watched or on screen time for my babies.

25. I also limit tv, screen and table time for my babies.

26. Similarly often times screen time, iPad and tablet are allowed as after all   work is done or as a award for my babies.

27. I maintain a set but reasonably flexible routine and schedule for my babies.

28. I strive to maintain a balanced schedule and routine for my babies.

29. I strive to facilitate and foster a good relationship for my babies with their grandparents.

30. I in choosing the toys I purchase for my babies they are fun and educational that can grow with my babies.

31. I also try to facilitate and foster their relationships with their friends with   lots of playdates.

32. With my babies we play and make up games tougher to play.

33. As a mommy I use phrases Because I said so/I told you too.

34. I strive to encourage my babies to be givers and sharers.

35. I strive to help problem solve and create opportunities for my babies to learn how to solve their problems and resolve conflict.

36. As a mommy I never use words like 'you are being bad' or 'your being a brat's fill int he blank. Instead I will say 'you are being interesting right now and not making good/green choices'.

37. When speaking to my babies I strive to be extremely careful in my word choice.

38. I set rules, limits, boundaries and enforce them with my babies.

39. I get my babies to school, actives and places we go on time.

40. I teach my babies to prepare for school the next day by what we do in our morning and evening routines.

41. I will ask my babies how their days were.

42. My babies did and do abcmouse.com.

43. I demonstrate that I respect their boundaries.

44. I as a mommy strive to find time for myself.

45. I as a mommy strive to make sure I do self care for myself.

46. I as a mommy strive to take my sips, take my breath and go on as I continue to travel through my own journey as a mommy.

Ways to Take Our Sips, Breaths and Go....to Relax, Refresh and Rejuvenate

Explore, Discovery, Learn and Journey through Your own Motherhood

These are simply a list of ideas that I have done or that would be a good suggested for you as a mommy to use or do to help finding ways for you to get your sips and breathes in your own journey as a mommy. Finding these moments can be found in the simple every day ways and daily moments. Or it can also be found in the big ways or opportunities in our journey as mommies. These opportunities and suggestion can be the daily grace we need or the much-needed break and time away to helps as moms. These things are way for us to take or our need sea have attention given to our own self care. These chances, suggestion and opportunities also, or at least as I found to be the case for me, can give us the opportunity to catch our breath, stay balanced and recenter ourselves as moms traveling through this journey of motherhood. We as mommies should strive to ensure that we and each of you get your moments, opportunities to have ways for your Me O'clocks and moment of time away for yourself. In doing this we are giving ourselves, our baby and families a happier, sander and best version of ourselves. Explore and discover what are the ways you can do this for yourself and in your own journey as a mommy.

Ways to Take Our Sips, Breaths and Go....
to Relax, Refresh and Rejuvenate

1. Get much needed rest and sleep.

2. Feed and fuel your body and mind by getting your meals/snacks.

3. Feed and fuel your body, mind and spirit by getting your sips of your favorite drinks.

4. Take the time to fuel your body by exercising through whatever means and method you like.

5. Take the time to nourish your mind through yoga and meditation.

6. Take the time to nourish your spirit and soul through spiritual exercise and particle.

7. Take the time to nourish your mind, spirit and time with your tribe and girlfriends.

8. Take the time to nourish you, your mind, spirit, and your family by spending and investing in those who you love and who love you.

9. Take time to nourish you and your partner, spouse, significant another who is in this parenting thing with you as you travel through your motherhood.

10. Nourish your heart, spirit and soul and your babies by taking the time to cherish, treasure, hold dear, and

remember the sweet tenderness of your babies and your journey through motherhood.

11. Take time for yourself on a regular basis.

12. Learn the intention to make a habit of scheduling these things for yourself.

13. Learn the intention of making these ways of nourishing you, your self care, your body, mind, heart, spirit and soul a priority in your journey as a mommy.

14. Remember the things/hobbies that you take joy in that you can do for yourself even just a little.

15. Lean and implant the value of no and boundaries and protection your time and the priority of doing so in your journey.

16. Be intentional in finding the joy in things and treasuring them.

17. Be intentional in treasuring your journey and your motherhood.

18. Be intentional of these things for your sense of balance, centeredness, focus, sanity and ability to be the mommy you want to be as you travel this journey.

19. Remember to show your beautifully brilliant rainbow of mommy true colors.

20. May you strive to learn, grow and discover and enjoy this amazing most special journey of a lifetime we call motherhood.

Appendix C
List of Resources for the Journey Ahead

Purpose of Appendix C

The purpose of this appendix C is to offer some information and good reads for us fellow mommies as we travel our journeys. Yes there are no instruction manuals for this thing we call motherhood. Yes we are becoming bit by bit less virginal mamas that we once were as we started this journey. Yes we are finding our own mama voice, learning how to hear and listen to our own voice. Yes as we travel we are becoming more and more our own amazing expert for ourselves, our children and our family as we continue on this journey. Even the most expert mommies need insight into this thing we call motherhood from time to time. So whether you are a complete virgin in motherhood or most seasoned and the very best expert in your motherhood journey I offer these resources to aid my fellow travelers as we all keep taking our sips, breaths and go forward traveling through motherhood.

Resources for the journey ahead

1.Resources from Focus on the Family
https://www.focusonthefamily.com/

2.Resources by Grace based Parenting
https://gracebasedparenting.com/

3.The Power of the Parenting by Stormie Omartian
https://www.stormieomartian.com/

4. The 5 Love Languages for Children by Gary Chapman
https://www.5lovelanguages.com/

5. Strong and Kind by Korie Robertson & Chrys Howard
http://www.strongandkindbook.com/

6. Motherly
https://www.mother.ly/

7. Books by Jed Jurchenko
http://www.coffeeshopconversations.com/

About the Author

Michaela S. Cox has always had a great love and passion for writing. Michaela was first Published in 2011 with her book entitled Heartfelt Meditations: A Collection of Poetry Inspired by cherish Scriptures. Also in 2016 Michaela has been published in Light and Life publication. Michaela is also the Author the first book in her series on her own journey through motherhood entitled Take a Sip, Take a Breath and Go.... A Journey Through Motherhood. Michaela is passionate about sharing her message and story especially her own journey as a mama. Michaela is a mother to her beautiful amazing children and has been traveling on her own journey through motherhood for the nine years and counting. Another aspect that makes Michaela's story and message unique is that Michaela has been (originally at birth blind) visually impaired/legally blind her entire life. Michaela wishes very much to share all her observations, discoveries, experiences and lessons learned with her fellow travels through motherhood. Michaela has her B.A in sociology and double minors in English and History. As Michaela entered into mothered and while traveling her first five years of her journey through motherhood she earned her M.A. in Political Science and graduate certificate in Ancient/Classical History from American Public University.

Michaela is originally from Houston, Texas. Michaela and her two children currently reside in Louisiana. In her free time

Michaela enjoys her journey with her babies and hanging with her fabulous friends. Also Michaela has great interest and passion in matters related to her faith. Michaela also enjoys reading, journaling and working on Shutterfly.com

Continue the Journey
with Michaela

If you enjoyed this book I would love if you would leave a review. Your encouragement is an immense and enormous encouragement to me and it helps books like this get noticed. It only takes a quick minute, and every review is greatly appreciated. Also if you want to keep in touch and see where to find Michaela and follow the latest

Michaela Earlier Publication

Take a Sip, Take a Breathe and Go....
A Journey through Motherhood

amazon.com

Heartfelt Mediations: A Collection of Poetry
Inspired by Cherished Scriptures

Can be found on the following websites:
amazon.com
BN.com
IUNiverse.com

Contact Michaela S. Cox:

Email: nowisee779@yahoo.com

Facebook: https://www.facebook.com/Heartfelt-Meditations -by-Michaela-S-Cox-326674074197797/

Twitter: https://twitter.com/nowisee779?s=09

Instagram: @nowisee779

Wordpress: https://myheartfeltmeditations.blog/

A word of Heartfelt Gratitude

A Heartfelt Thanks to:

My Heavenly Father

I would like express my most profound and heartfelt thanks to first and foremost to My Heavenly Father and my Lord and Savior Jesus Christ for being with me in all that I do and always being there for me no matter where my life's journey has taken me.

To My Beautiful Babies

I would like to express my most profound and heartfelt thanks to my beautiful and amazing babies. Without them I wouldn't have become a mommy and started to travel my own journey into motherhood. I love you my precious amazing treasures with all my heart and with every breath I take. I love you always and forever to the moon and back.

To My Friends & Family

Also I would like to express my most profound heartfelt thanks to my friend and family. I thank them who have always been there for me over the years in all that i have done and do with their amazing heartfelt kind support, encouragement and love. Thanks for always be there for me cheering me on always

My Editor, Cover Designer & Formatter

MS. Elaine Roughton my amazing Editor
Mrs. Andrea Jackson my incredible graphic designer at andrealjacksondesgins@gmail.com
Mrs. Debbie Lum my fantastic formatter at debbie.debbiestevenlum.com

Chandler Bolt & Self Publishing School

Chandler Bolt founder of Self Publishing School
Jed Jurchenko (SPS Coach)
The whole and entire Self Publishing program by Chandler Bolt and the whole SPS community.

Find, See and Check out Chandler Bolt's Self Publishing School:
https://self-publishingschool.com/
https://www.facebook.com/chandler.bolt1
https://www.youtube.com/chandlerboltofficial
https://www.youtube.com/selfpublishingschool

Thumbs Up or Thumbs Down

A most profound, sincere and heartfelt thanks beyond words for purchasing this book. I would love to hear from you! Your feedback not only helps me grow as a writer but also help me to share my message and story with others by getting books into the hands who may learn, grow, and Benefit from them the most. Online reviews are on of the most significant ways independent authors like me connect with new readers. Another way to achieve this is by those who read this help spread the word and pass this on to others.

If you loved the book, could you please share your experience and pass it on to others who may also benefit form this book.

Leaving feedback is as easy as answering any of these questions:

- What did you like about the book?

- What is your most valuable take away from the book?

- What have you done differently or what will you do differently Because of what you have read?

- To whom will you recommend this book?

Of course, I'm looking for honest reviews, so if you have a minute to share your experience, good or bad, please consider leaving a review! Please also consider passing on to others about this book and help me get it to others so that many more can also learn and experience my message and story. I very much look forward to hearing from you.

Sincerely,

Michaela S. Cox

Made in the USA
Las Vegas, NV
05 November 2020

10580923R00125